Learning the Violin, Viola, Cello, and Bass Score

Book One

For individual study,
single-string classes, or
mixed-string classes

expanded edition

Piano accompaniment by MyAnna Harvey
method and parts by Cassia Harvey

CHP284

C. Harvey Publications

©2015 by C. Harvey Publications   All Rights Reserved.

www.charveypublications.com

Instrumental Books: Warmup, Page 2

Violin

Warmup Exercise for the Beginning of Class

0 1 2 3 4 3 2 1

0 1 2 3 4 3 2 1

0 1 2 3 4 3 2 1

0 1 2 3 4 3 2 1

0

Play this exercise on all four strings.
Use it as a warmup every time you play.

Viola

Warmup Exercise for the Beginning of Class

0 1 2 3 4 3 2 1

0 1 2 3 4 3 2 1

0 1 2 3 4 3 2 1

0 1 2 3 4 3 2 1

0

Play this exercise on all four strings.
Use it as a warmup every time you play.

Cello

Warmup Exercise for the Beginning of Class

0 1 3 4 3 4 3 1

0 1 3 4 3 4 3 1

0 1 3 4 3 4 3 1

0 1 3 4 3 4 3 1

0

Play this exercise on all four strings.
Use it as a warmup every time you play.

Bass

Warmup Exercise for the Beginning of Class

0 1 4 1 4 1 4 1

0 1 4 1 4 1 4 1

0 1 4 1 4 1 4 1

0 1 4 1 4 1 4 1

0

Play this exercise on all four strings.
Use it as a warmup every time you play.

©2015 C. Harvey Publications All Rights Reserved.

Piano Accompaniments for Warmup, Page 2

Violin and Bass play the Warmup on the E string.

Violin, Viola, Cello, and Bass play the Warmup on the A string.

Violin, Viola, Cello, and Bass play the Warmup on the D string.

Violin, Viola, Cello, and Bass play the Warmup on the G string.

Learning the Violin, Viola, Cello, and Bass Score, Book One

Viola and Cello play the Warmup on the C string.

Instrumental Books: #1, Page 3

1. Parts of the Violin and Bow

VIOLIN

1. scroll
2. peg box
3. pegs
4. nut
5. neck
6. fingerboard
7. sides
8. f holes
9. bridge
10. tailpiece
11. fine tuners

Chinrest or sponge goes here.

Bow — tip, stick, screw, horsehair, frog

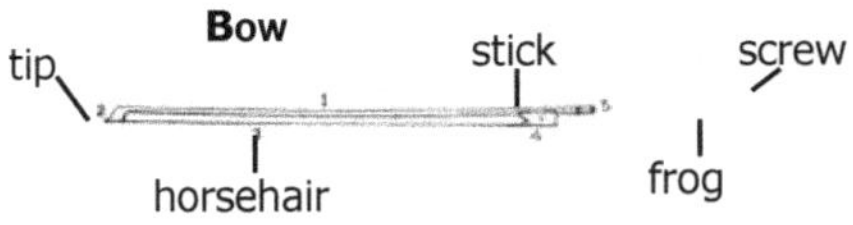

1. Parts of the Viola and Bow

VIOLA

1. scroll
2. peg box
3. pegs
4. nut
5. neck
6. fingerboard
7. sides
8. f holes
9. bridge
10. tailpiece
11. fine tuners

Chinrest or sponge goes here.

Bow — tip, stick, screw, horsehair, frog

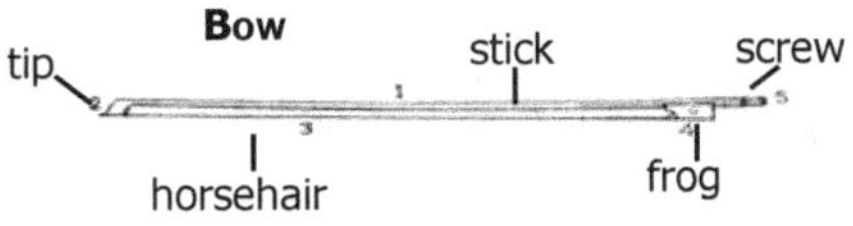

1. Parts of the Cello and Bow

CELLO

1. scroll
2. peg box
3. pegs
4. nut
5. neck
6. fingerboard
7. sides
8. f holes
9. bridge
10. tailpiece
11. fine tuners
12. endpin

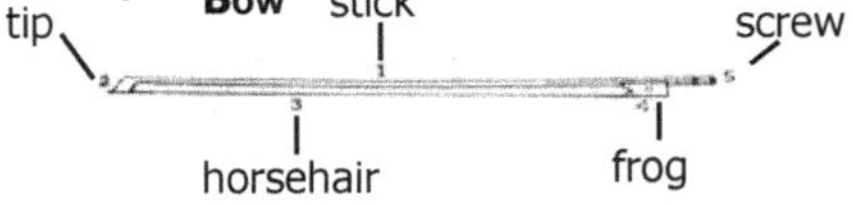

Bow — tip, stick, screw, horsehair, frog

1. Parts of the Bass and Bow

BASS

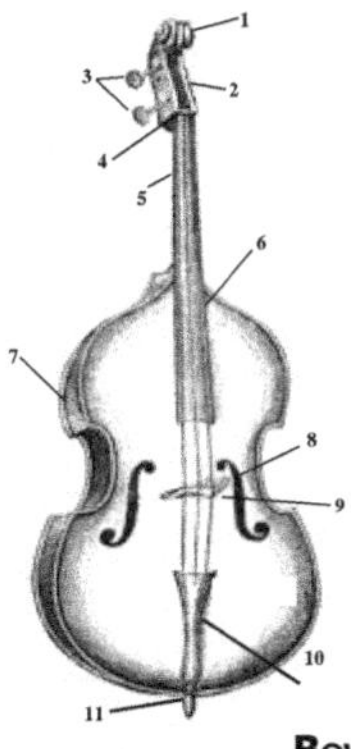

1. scroll
2. peg box
3. pegs
4. nut
5. neck
6. fingerboard
7. sides
8. f holes
9. bridge
10. tailpiece
11. endpin

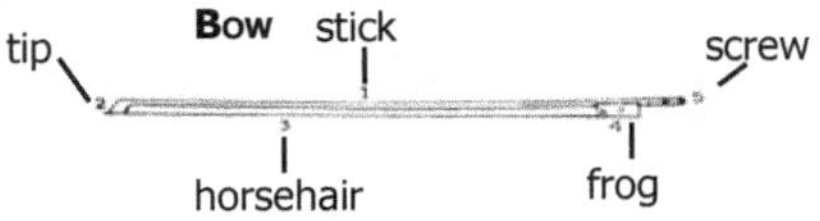

Bow — tip, stick, screw, horsehair, frog

©2015 C. Harvey Publications All Rights Reserved.

Instrumental Books: #2, Page 4

2. Taking care of the Violin (Viola, Cello, Bass)

Keep your violin away from pets.

Don't let the violin drop (or the bow).

The wood is very fragile.

No water on the violin or bow.

Keep the violin off of heaters and away from open windows.

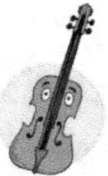

Instrumental Books: #3, Page 5

3. Taking care of the Bow

Don't touch the bow hair!

Righty-tighty: To tighten the bow, turn the screw to the right.

Lefty-loosey: To loosen the bow, turn the screw to the left.

Always loosen the bow when you are finished playing.

Keep the violin and bow up off the floor.

©2015 C. Harvey Publications All Rights Reserved.

Instrumental Books: #4, Page 6

Violin
4. The Open Strings

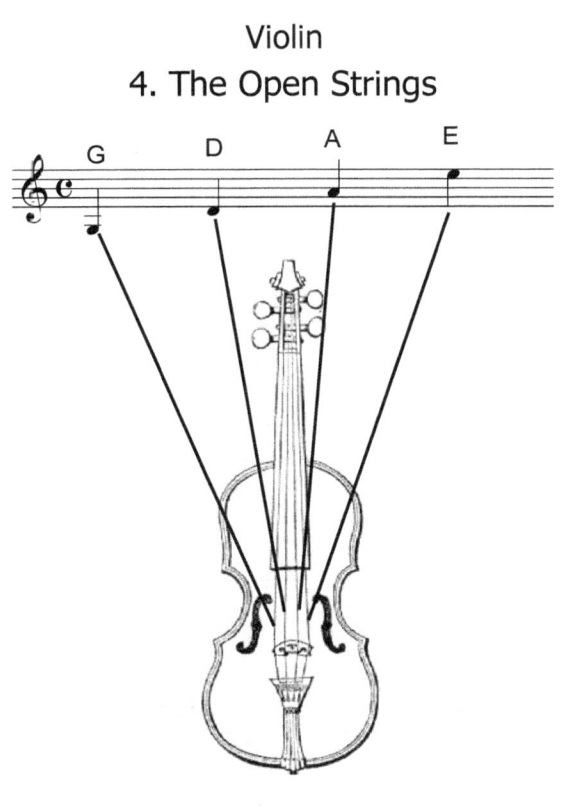

Viola
4. The Open Strings

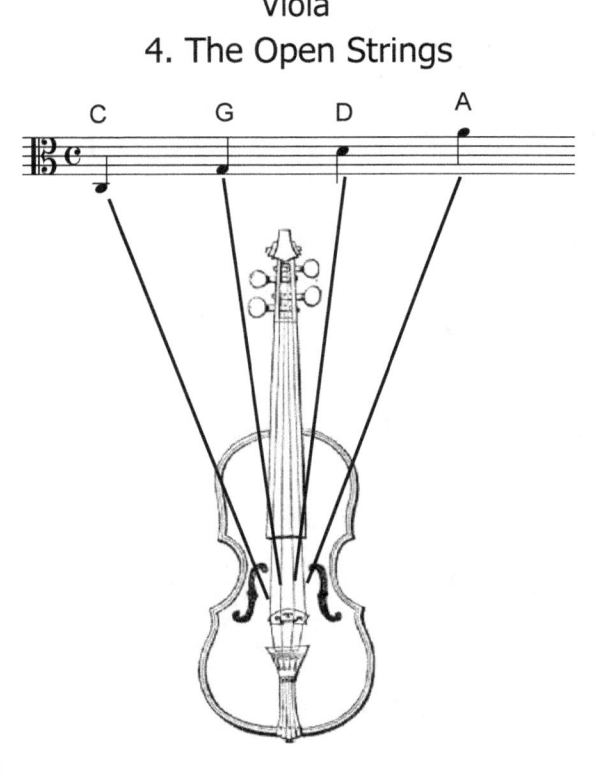

Cello
4. The Open Strings

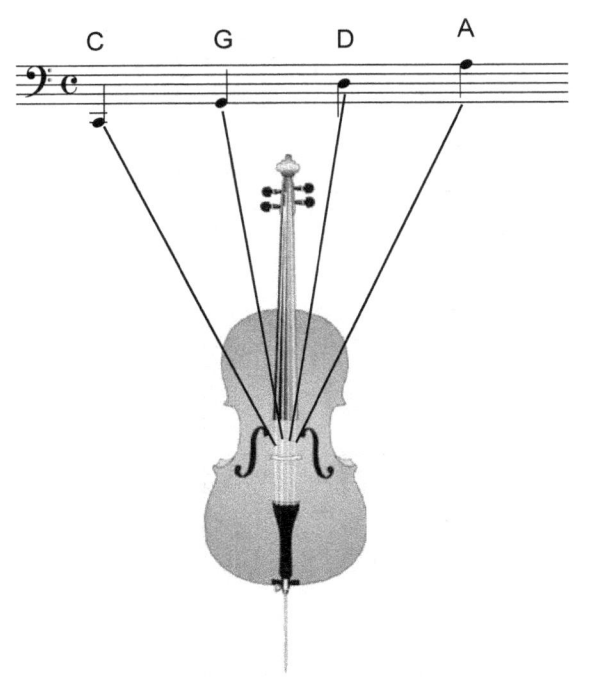

Bass
4. The Open Strings

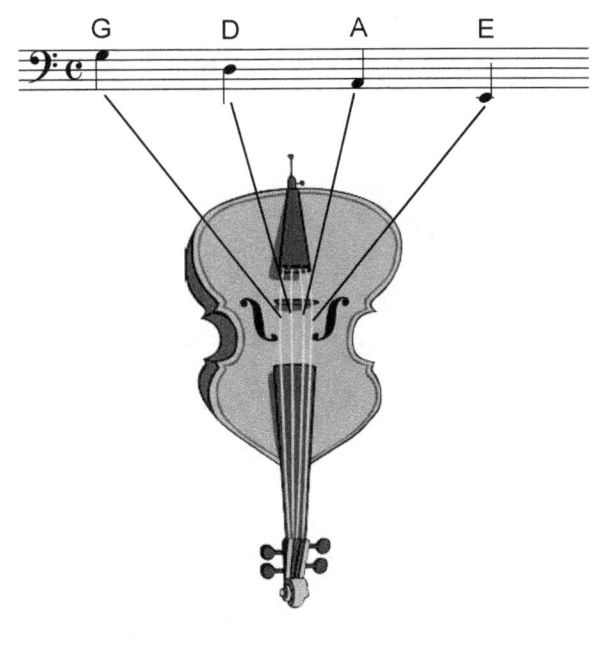

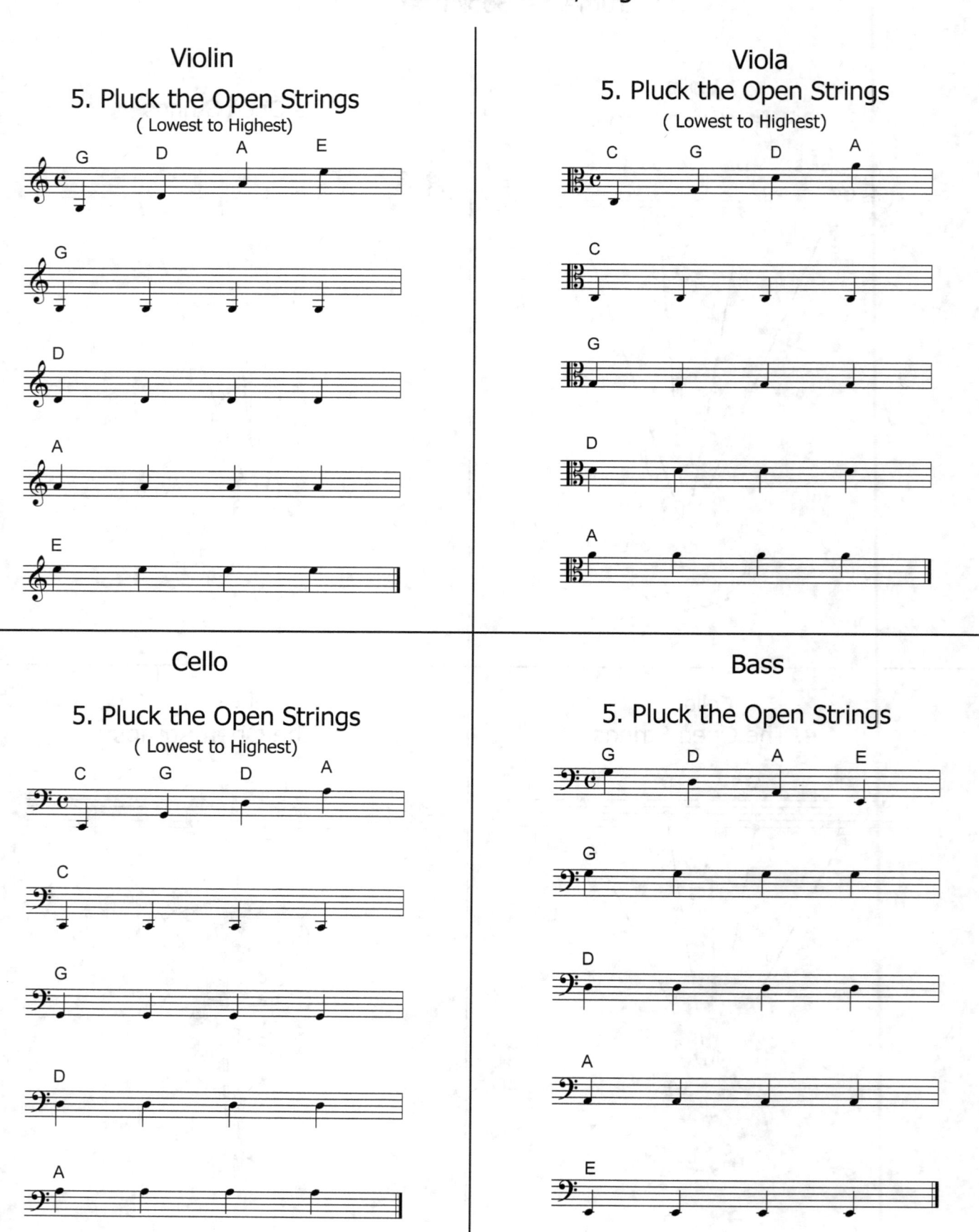

Learning the Violin, Viola, Cello, and Bass Score, Book One

Instrumental Books: #5, Page 7
Piano Accompaniment

5. Pluck the Open Strings

©2015 C. Harvey Publications: All Rights Reserved.

Instrumental Books: #6, Page 8

Violin
6. Open String Song

play with long bows, from the frog to the tip

GGGG   DDDD   AAAA   EEEE

EEEE   AAAA   DDDD   GGGG

GG DD AA EE EE AA DD GG

GDGD   DADA   AEAE   EADG

Viola
6. Open String Song

play with long bows, from the frog to the tip

CCCC   GGGG   DDDD   AAAA

AAAA   DDDD   GGGG   CCCC

CC GG DD AA AA DD GG CC

CGCG   GDGD   DADA   ADGC

Cello
6. Open String Song

play with long bows, from the frog to the tip

CCCC   GGGG   DDDD   AAAA

AAAA   DDDD   GGGG   CCCC

CC GG DD AA AA DD GG CC

CGCG   GDGD   DADA   ADGC

Bass
6. Open String Song

play with long bows, from the frog to the tip

GGGG   DDDD   AAAA   EEEE

EEEE   AAAA   DDDD   GGGG

GG DD AA EE EE AA DD GG

GDGD   DADA   AEAE   EADG

©2015 C. Harvey Publications All Rights Reserved.

Learning the Violin, Viola, Cello, and Bass Score, Book One

Instrumental Books: #6, Page 8
Piano Accompaniment

6. Open String Song

©2015 C. Harvey Publications All Rights Reserved.

Instrumental Books: #7, Page 9

Violin
7. Mississippi Hot Dog
4 short bows and 2 long bows

Play the rhythm "Mississippi Hot Dog" on each note:

G G D D   A A E E

G D A E   E A D G

G D   D A   A E   E A

Viola
7. Mississippi Hot Dog
4 short bows and 2 long bows

Play the rhythm "Mississippi Hot Dog" on each note:

C C G G   D D A A

C G D A   A D G C

C G   G D   D A   A D

Cello
7. Mississippi Hot Dog
4 short bows and 2 long bows

Play the rhythm "Mississippi Hot Dog" on each note:

C C G G   D D A A

C G D A   A D G C

C G   G D   D A   A D

Bass
7. Mississippi Hot Dog
4 short bows and 2 long bows

Play the rhythm "Mississippi Hot Dog" on each note:

G G D D   A A E E

G D A E   E A D G

G D   D A   A E   E A

©2015 C. Harvey Publications All Rights Reserved.

This page left blank
to facilitate page turns.

14   Learning the Violin, Viola, Cello, and Bass Score, Book One

Instrumental Books: #7, Page 9
Piano Accompaniment

7. Mississippi Hot Dog

©2015 C. Harvey Publications All Rights Reserved.

Learning the Violin, Viola, Cello, and Bass Score, Book One

(Instrumental Books: #7, Page 9
Piano Accompaniment cont.)

©2015 C. Harvey Publications All Rights Reserved.

16 — Learning the Violin, Viola, Cello, and Bass Score, Book One

Instrumental Books: #8, Page 10

Violin
8. Blueberry Song: Long-Short-Short

G - GG	G - GG
D - DD	D - DD
A - AA	A - AA
E - EE	E - EE
A - AA	A - AA
D - DD	D - DD

Viola
8. Blueberry Song: Long-Short Short

C - CC	C - CC
G - GG	G - GG
D - DD	D - DD
A - AA	A - AA
D - DD	D - DD
G - GG	G - GG

Cello
8. Blueberry Song: Long-Short Short

C - CC	C - CC
G - GG	G - GG
D - DD	D - DD
A - AA	A - AA
D - DD	D - DD
G - GG	G - GG

Bass
8. Blueberry Song: Long-Short-Short

G - GG	G - GG
D - DD	D - DD
A - AA	A - AA
E - EE	E - EE
A - AA	A - AA
D - DD	D - DD

8. Blueberry Song: Long-Short Short

©2015 C. Harvey Publications All Rights Reserved.

Learning the Violin, Viola, Cello, and Bass Score, Book One

Instrumental Books: #9, Page 11

Violin

9. Speedy Open Strings

AAAA EEEE

AAAA DDDD

GGGG DDDD

AAEE AAEE

AADD AADD

GGDD GGDD

Viola

9. Speedy Open Strings

DDDD AAAA

DDDD GGGG

CCCC GGGG

DDAA DDAA

DDGG DDGG

CCGG CCGG

Cello

9. Speedy Open Strings

DDDD AAAA

DDDD GGGG

CCCC GGGG

DDAA DDAA

DDGG DDGG

CCGG CCGG

Bass

9. Speedy Open Strings

AAAA EEEE

AAAA DDDD

GGGG DDDD

AAEE AAEE

AADD AADD

GGDD GGDD

9. Speedy Open Strings

©2015 C. Harvey Publications All Rights Reserved.

Instrumental Books: #10, Page 12

Violin
10. The Finger Numbers

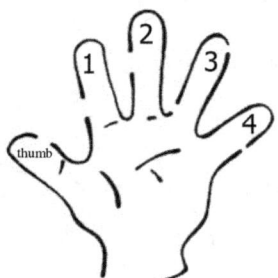

Using the Fingers

0 is for open string
1 is for first finger
2 is for second finger
3 is for third finger
4 is for fourth finger
The thumb goes under the neck of the violin.

Viola
10. The Finger Numbers

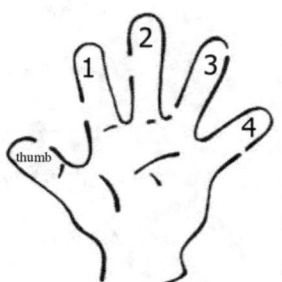

Using the Fingers

0 is for open string
1 is for first finger
2 is for second finger
3 is for third finger
4 is for fourth finger
The thumb goes under the neck of the viola.

Cello
10. The Finger Numbers

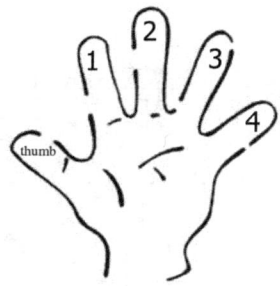

Using the Fingers

0 is for open string
1 is for first finger
2 is for second finger
3 is for third finger
4 is for fourth finger
The thumb goes under the neck of the cello.

Bass
10. The Finger Numbers

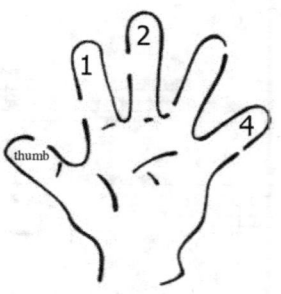

Using the Fingers

0 is for open string
1 is for first finger
2 is for second finger
4 is for fourth finger
The thumb goes under the neck of the bass.

©2015 C. Harvey Publications All Rights Reserved.

This page left blank
to facilitate page turns.

Instrumental Books: #11, Page 13: **Top**

Violin

11. First Finger Song

0000   1111   0000   1111

00 11 00 11   1111   0000

String Class: Play on the A string or the D string.
Solo: Can be played on all 4 strings.

Viola

11. First Finger Song

0000   1111   0000   1111

00 11 00 11   1111   0000

String Class: Play on the A string or D string.
Solo: Can be played on all 4 strings.

Cello

11. First Finger Song

0000   1111   0000   1111

00 11 00 11   1111   0000

String Class: Play on the A string or D string.
Solo: Can be played on all 4 strings.

Bass

11. First Finger Song

0000   1111   0000   1111

00 11 00 11   1111   0000

String Class: Play on the A string or D string.
Solo: Can be played on all 4 strings.

©2015 C. Harvey Publications All Rights Reserved.

Learning the Violin, Viola, Cello, and Bass Score, Book One

Instrumental Books: #11, Page 13: **Top**
Piano Accompaniment

11. First Finger Song (on A)

11b. First Finger Song (on D)

©2015 C. Harvey Publications All Rights Reserved.

Instrumental Books: #12, Page 13: **Bottom**

Violin

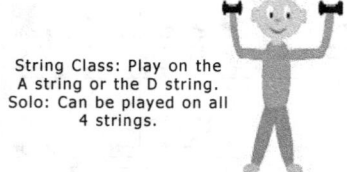

String Class: Play on the A string or the D string.
Solo: Can be played on all 4 strings.

12. First Finger Challenge

0011	0011	0000	1111
0011	1100	1111	0000
0101	0000	0101	0000

Viola

String Class: Play on the A string or D string.
Solo: Can be played on all 4 strings.

12. First Finger Challenge

0011	0011	0000	1111
0011	1100	1111	0000
0101	0000	0101	0000

Cello

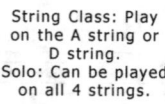

String Class: Play on the A string or D string.
Solo: Can be played on all 4 strings.

12. First Finger Challenge

0011	0011	0000	1111
0011	1100	1111	0000
0101	0000	0101	0000

Bass

String Class: Play on the A string or D string.
Solo: Can be played on all 4 strings.

12. First Finger Challenge

0011	0011	0000	1111
0011	1100	1111	0000
0101	0000	0101	0000

©2015 C. Harvey Publications All Rights Reserved.

Learning the Violin, Viola, Cello, and Bass Score, Book One

Instrumental Books: #12, Page 13: **Bottom**
Piano Accompaniment

12. First Finger Challenge (on A)

12b. First Finger Challenge (on D)

©2015 C. Harvey Publications All Rights Reserved.

Instrumental Books: #13, Page 14: **Top**

Violin	Viola
13. Second Finger Song	13. Second Finger Song
0000 1111 2222 1111	0000 1111 2222 1111
0000 1111 2222 1111	0000 1111 2222 1111
00 11 22 11 00 11 22 11 00	00 11 22 11 00 11 22 11 00

Cello	Bass
13. Third Finger Song	13. Fourth Finger Song
0000 1111 3333 1111	0000 1111 4444 1111
0000 1111 3333 1111	0000 1111 4444 1111
00 11 33 11 00 11 33 11 00	00 11 44 11 00 11 44 11 00

13. Second, Third, Fourth Finger Song (on A)

Learning the Violin, Viola, Cello, and Bass Score, Book One   25

Instrumental Books: #13, Page 14: **Top**
Piano Accompaniment

13b. Second, Third, Fourth Finger Song (on D)

©2015 C. Harvey Publications All Rights Reserved.

Instrumental Books: #14, Page 14: Bottom

Violin

String Class: Play on the A string or the D string.
Solo: Can be played on all 4 strings.

14. Second Finger Challenge!

11 00 11 22 11 22 1111

22 11 2121 2121 0000

Viola

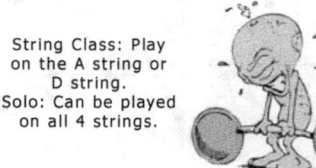

String Class: Play on the A string or D string.
Solo: Can be played on all 4 strings.

14. Second Finger Challenge!

11 00 11 22 11 22 1111

22 11 2121 2121 0000

Cello

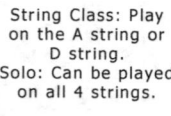 

String Class: Play on the A string or D string.
Solo: Can be played on all 4 strings.

14. Third Finger Challenge!

11 00 11 33 11 33 1111

33 11 3131 3131 0000

Bass

String Class: Play on the A string or D string.
Solo: Can be played on all 4 strings.

14. Fourth Finger Challenge!

11 00 11 44 11 44 1111

44 11 4141 4141 0000

Learning the Violin, Viola, Cello, and Bass Score, Book One

Instrumental Books: #14, Page 14: **Bottom**
Piano Accompaniment

14. Second, Third, Fourth Finger Challenge (on A)

14b. Second, Third, Fourth Finger Challenge (on D)

©2015 C. Harvey Publications All Rights Reserved.

Instrumental Books: #15, Page 15: **Top**

Violin
15. Hot Cross Buns

210 -   210 -

0000   1111

210 -

String Class: Play on the A string or the D string.
Solo: Can be played on all 4 strings.

Viola
15. Hot Cross Buns

210 -   210 -

0000   1111

210 -

String Class: Play on the A string or D string.
Solo: Can be played on all 4 strings.

Cello
15. Hot Cross Buns

310 -   310 -

0000   1111

310 -

Bass
15. Hot Cross Buns

410 -   410 -

0000   1111

410 -

Instrumental Books: #15, Page 15: **Top**
Piano Accompaniment

15. Hot Cross Buns (on A)   15b. Hot Cross Buns (on D)

Instrumental Books: #15, Page 15: **Top**
Piano Accompaniment

15c. Hot Cross Buns (on G)

15d. Hot Cross Buns (on C)

15e. Hot Cross Buns (on E)

Instrumental Books: #16, Page 15: **Bottom**

Violin
16. Au clair de la Lune

0001   2 - 1 -   0211   0 ---

0001   2 - 1 -   0211   0 ---

Viola
16. Au clair de la Lune

0001   2 - 1 -   0211   0 ---

0001   2 - 1 -   0211   0 ---

Cello
16. Au clair de la Lune

0001   3 - 1 -   0311   0 ---

0001   3 - 1 -   0311   0 ---

Bass
16. Au clair de la Lune

0001   4 - 1 -   0411   0 ---

0001   4 - 1 -   0411   0 ---

Instrumental Books: #16, Page 15: **Bottom**
Piano Accompaniment

©2015 C. Harvey Publications All Rights Reserved.

Learning the Violin, Viola, Cello, and Bass Score, Book One

Instrumental Books: #16, Page 15: **Bottom**
Piano Accompaniment

Learning the Violin, Viola, Cello, and Bass Score, Book One

Instrumental Books: #17, Page 16

Violin

17. Mary Had a Little Lamb

2 1 0 1

2 2 2 -

1 1 1 -

2 2 2 -

2 1 0 1

2 2 2 2

1 1 2 1

0 - - -

String Class: Play on the A string or the D string.
Solo: Can be played on all 4 strings.

Viola

17. Mary Had a Little Lamb

2 1 0 1

2 2 2 -

1 1 1 -

2 2 2 -

2 1 0 1

2 2 2 2

1 1 2 1

0 - - -

String Class: Play on the A string or D string.
Solo: Can be played on all 4 strings.

Cello

17. Mary Had a Little Lamb

3 1 0 1

3 3 3 -

1 1 1 -

3 3 3 -

3 1 0 1

3 3 3 3

1 1 3 1

0 - - -

String Class: Play on the A string or D string.
Solo: Can be played on all 4 strings.

Bass

17. Mary Had a Little Lamb

4 1 0 1

4 4 4 -

1 1 1 -

4 4 4 -

4 1 0 1

4 4 4 4

1 1 4 1

0 - - -

String Class: Play on the A string or D string.
Solo: Can be played on all 4 strings.

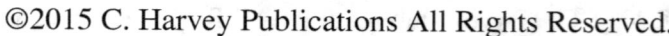

Instrumental Books: #17, Page 16
Piano Accompaniment

17. Mary Had a Little Lamb (on A)

17b. Mary Had a Little Lamb (on D)

Instrumental Books: #17, Page 16
Piano Accompaniment

17c. Mary Had a Little Lamb (on G)

17d. Mary Had a Little Lamb (on C)

Learning the Violin, Viola, Cello, and Bass Score, Book One

Instrumental Books: #17, Page 16
Piano Accompaniment

17e. Mary Had a Little Lamb (on E)

©2015 C. Harvey Publications All Rights Reserved.

Instrumental Books: #18, Page 17: **Top**

Violin
18. Third Finger Song

0000   1111   2222   3333

2222   3333   2222   1111

00 11 22 33 22 33 22 11 00

Viola
18. Third Finger Song

0000   1111   2222   3333

2222   3333   2222   1111

00 11 22 33 22 33 22 11 00

String Class: Play on the A string or the D string.
Solo: Can be played on all 4 strings.

Cello
18. Fourth Finger Song

0000   1111   3333   4444

3333   4444   3333   1111

00 11 33 44 33 44 33 11 00

Bass
18. Another Fourth Finger Song

0000   1111   4444   1111

4444   1111   4444   1111

00 11 44 11 44 11 44 11 00

18. Third, Fourth Finger Song (on A)

©2015 C. Harvey Publications All Rights Reserved.

Learning the Violin, Viola, Cello, and Bass Score, Book One

Instrumental Books: #18, Page 17: **Top**
Piano Accompaniment

18b. Third, Fourth Finger Song (on D)

©2015 C. Harvey Publications All Rights Reserved.

Instrumental Books: #19, Page 17: **Bottom**

Violin

String Class: Play on the A string or the D string.
Solo: Can be played on all 4 strings.

19. Third Finger Challenge!

11 22 33 22 11 22 33 22

22 33 21 21 00 11 23 23

Viola

String Class: Play on the A string or D string.
Solo: Can be played on all 4 strings.

19. Third Finger Challenge!

11 22 33 22 11 22 33 22

22 33 21 21 00 11 23 23

Cello

String Class: Play on the A string or D string.
Solo: Can be played on all 4 strings.

19. Fourth Finger Challenge!

11 33 44 33 11 33 44 33

33 44 31 31 00 11 34 34

Bass

String Class: Play on the A string or D string.
Solo: Can be played on all 4 strings.

19. Another Fourth Finger Challenge!

11 44 11 44 11 44 11 44

44 11 41 41 00 11 41 41

Instrumental Books: #19, Page 17: **Bottom**
Piano Accompaniment

19. Third, Fourth Finger Challenge (on A)

19b. Third, Fourth Finger Challenge (on D)

Instrumental Books: #20, Page 18

Violin
20. Finger Training

0 1 2 3 4 3 4 3

4 3 2 1 0 1 0 1

0 1 2 3 4 3 4 3

4 3 2 1 0 1 0 1

2 3 2 3 2 1 2 1 0

String Class: Play on the D string.
Solo: Can be played on all 4 strings.

Viola
20. Finger Training

0 1 2 3 4 3 4 3

4 3 2 1 0 1 0 1

0 1 2 3 4 3 4 3

4 3 2 1 0 1 0 1

2 3 2 3 2 1 2 1 0

String Class: Play on the D string.
Solo: Can be played on all 4 strings.

Cello
20. Finger Training

0 1 3 4 3 4 3 4

3 4 3 1 0 1 0 1

0 1 3 4 3 4 3 4

3 4 3 1 0 1 0 1

3 4 3 4 3 1 3 1 0

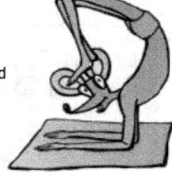

String Class: Play on the A string or D string.
Solo: Can be played on all 4 strings.

Bass
20. Finger Training

D string | G string
0 1 4 0 1 0 1 0

G string | D string
1 0 4 1 0 1 0 1

D string | G string
0 1 4 0 1 0 1 0

G string | D string
1 0 4 1 0 1 0 1

D string
4 1 4 1 4 1 4 1 0

©2015 C. Harvey Publications All Rights Reserved.

Learning the Violin, Viola, Cello, and Bass Score, Book One   41

Instrumental Books: #20, Page 18
Piano Accompaniment

20. Finger Training (on D to play together)

©2015 C. Harvey Publications All Rights Reserved.

Instrumental Books: #21a, Page 19
(Piano accompaniment on Page 44)

Violin

21a. Ode to Joy

String Class: Start on the D string.
Solo: Start on the A string.   Beethoven

2 2 3 4 4 3 2 1

0 0 1 2 2 1 1 -

2 2 3 4 4 3 2 1

0 0 1 2 1 0 0 -

Can you figure out the rest?

Viola

21a. Ode to Joy

If playing this in a class, start on the D string.   Beethoven

2 2 3 4 4 3 2 1

0 0 1 2 2 1 1 -

2 2 3 4 4 3 2 1

0 0 1 2 1 0 0 -

Can you figure out the rest?

Cello

21a. Ode to Joy

Start on the D string.
"A" means open A string.   Beethoven

3 3 4 A A 4 3 1

0 0 1 3 3 1 1 -

3 3 4 A A 4 3 1

0 0 1 3 1 0 0 -

Can you figure out the rest?

Bass

21a. Ode to Joy

Beethoven

| D string | G string | D string |
| 4 4 | 0 1 1 0 | 4 1 |

0 0 1 4 4 1 1 -

| G string | D string |
| 4 4 0 1 | 1 0 4 1 |

0 0 1 4 1 0 0 -

Can you figure out the rest?

©2015 C. Harvey Publications All Rights Reserved.

Learning the Violin, Viola, Cello, and Bass Score, Book One

Instrumental Books: #21b, Page 20
(Piano accompaniment on Page 45)

Violin

21b. Special Challenge:
Ode to Joy, Second Part

Start on the D string.

1 1 2 0   1 2 3 2 0

1 2 3 2 1   0 1 | 1 - | *Play this on the G String*

2 2 3 4   4 3 2 1

0 0 1 2   1 - 0 0

Viola

21b. Special Challenge:
Ode to Joy, Second Part

Start on the D string.

1 1 2 0   1 2 3 2 0

1 2 3 2 1   0 1 | 1 - | *Play this on the G String*

2 2 3 4   4 3 2 1

0 0 1 2   1 - 0 0

Cello

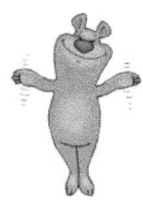

21b. Special Challenge:
Ode to Joy, Second Part

Start on the D string.

1 1 3 0   1 3 4 3 0

1 3 4 3 1   0 1 | 1 - | *Play this on the G String*

3 3 4 A   A 4 3 1

0 0 1 3   1 - 0 0

Bass

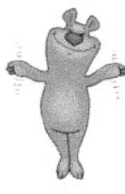

21b. Special Challenge:
Ode to Joy, Second Part

D string	G string / D string
1 1 4 0	1 4 0 4 0

G string / D string	Open A string
1 4 0 4 1 0 1	0 -

D string	G string	D string
4 4	0 1 1 0	4 1

0 0 1 4   1 - 0 0

©2015 C. Harvey Publications All Rights Reserved.

Instrumental Books: #21a, Page 19
Piano Accompaniment

21a. Ode to Joy (on D to play together)

Beethoven, arr. Harvey

21b. Special Challenge: Ode to Joy, Second Part

Learning the Violin, Viola, Cello, and Bass Score, Book One

Instrumental Books: #21b, Page 20
Piano Accompaniment

Ode to Joy on A and E (for Violins and Violas)

Beethoven, arr. Harvey

Special Challenge: Ode to Joy, Second Part

©2015 C. Harvey Publications All Rights Reserved.

Violin

22. Rests

This sign is called a quarter rest:

𝄽

When you see a rest like this, stop playing and count to 1 before playing again.

 String Class: Play on the A string or the D string.
Solo: Can be played on all 4 strings.

23. Au clair de la Lune

0 0 0 1 2 𝄽 1 𝄽

0 2 1 1 0 𝄽 𝄽 𝄽
Repeat

Viola

22. Rests

This sign is called a quarter rest:

𝄽

When you see a rest like this, stop playing and count to 1 before playing again.

 String Class: Play on the A string or the D string.
Solo: Can be played on all 4 strings.

23. Au clair de la Lune

0 0 0 1 2 𝄽 1 𝄽

0 2 1 1 0 𝄽 𝄽 𝄽
Repeat

Cello

22. Rests

This sign is called a quarter rest:

𝄽

When you see a rest like this, stop playing and count to 1 before playing again.

 String Class: Play on the A string or the D string.
Solo: Can be played on all 4 strings.

23. Au clair de la Lune

0 0 0 1 3 𝄽 1 𝄽

0 3 1 1 0 𝄽 𝄽 𝄽
Repeat

Bass

22. Rests

This sign is called a quarter rest:

𝄽

When you see a rest like this, stop playing and count to 1 before playing again.

 String Class: Play on the A string or the D string.
Solo: Can be played on all 4 strings.

23. Au clair de la Lune

0 0 0 1 4 𝄽 1 𝄽

0 4 1 1 0 𝄽 𝄽 𝄽
Repeat

Instrumental Books: #23, Page 21
Piano Accompaniment

22. Rests

23. Au claire de la Lune (on D to play together)

Au claire de la Lune (on A for Violins, Violas, and Cellos)

Instrumental Books: #24, Page 22

Violin

Breaking the notes up

Now we break the notes up with a line: |

String Class: Play on the D string.
Solo: Can be played on all 4 strings.

24. Purcell's Rigaudon

3 3 2 1 | 0 𝄽 𝄽 𝄽

1 1 2 0 | 3 𝄽 0 𝄽

3 3 2 1 | 0 𝄽 𝄽 𝄽

1 1 2 0 | 3 𝄽 𝄽 𝄽

Viola

Breaking the notes up

Now we break the notes up with a line: |

String Class: Play on the D string.
Solo: Can be played on all 4 strings.

24. Purcell's Rigaudon

3 3 2 1 | 0 𝄽 𝄽 𝄽

1 1 2 0 | 3 𝄽 0 𝄽

3 3 2 1 | 0 𝄽 𝄽 𝄽

1 1 2 0 | 3 𝄽 𝄽 𝄽

Cello

Breaking the notes up

Now we break the notes up with a line: |

String Class: Play on the D string.
Solo: Can be played on all 4 strings.

24. Purcell's Rigaudon

4 4 3 1 | 0 𝄽 𝄽 𝄽

1 1 3 0 | 4 𝄽 0 𝄽

4 4 3 1 | 0 𝄽 𝄽 𝄽

1 1 3 0 | 4 𝄽 𝄽 𝄽

Bass

Breaking the notes up

Now we break the notes up with a line: |

24. Purcell's Rigaudon

G string | D string
0 0 4 1 | 0 𝄽 𝄽 𝄽

D string | G string | D string
1 1 4 0 | 0 𝄽 0 𝄽

G string | D string
0 0 4 1 | 0 𝄽 𝄽 𝄽

D string | G string
1 1 4 0 | 0 𝄽 𝄽 𝄽

Learning the Violin, Viola, Cello, and Bass Score, Book One

Instrumental Books: #24, Page 22
Piano Accompaniment

24. Purcell's Rigaudon (on D to play together)

Note: This is a great place to have the students stomp their feet (once for each rest).

Purcell's Rigaudon (on A for Violins, Violas, and Cellos)

©2015 C. Harvey Publications All Rights Reserved.

Instrumental Books: #25, Page 23: **Top**

Violin

25. A Regal March
(on the D String if playing in a class)

0012 | 3322 | 0012 | 1100

0012 | 3322 | 0012 | 1100

Viola

25. A Regal March
(on the D String if playing in a class)

0012 | 3322 | 0012 | 1100

0012 | 3322 | 0012 | 1100

Cello

25. A Regal March
(on the D String if playing in a class.)

0013 | 4433 | 0013 | 1100

0013 | 4433 | 0013 | 1100

Bass

25. A Regal March
(Start on the D String. "G" means open G.)

0014 | GG44 | 0014 | 1100

0014 | GG44 | 0014 | 1100

©2015 C. Harvey Publications All Rights Reserved.

Learning the Violin, Viola, Cello, and Bass Score, Book One

Instrumental Books: #25, Page 23: **Top**
Piano Accompaniment

25. A Regal March (on D to play together)

A Regal March (on A for Violins, Violas, and Cellos)

©2015 C. Harvey Publications All Rights Reserved.

Instrumental Books: #26, Page 23: **Bottom**

Violin

26. Three-Leaf Clover
(on the D String if playing in a class)

222 | 012 | 111 | 444
222 | 012 | 111 | 000
333 | 222 | 012 | 111
333 | 222 | 121 | 000

Viola

26. Three-Leaf Clover
(on the D String if playing in a class)

222 | 012 | 111 | 444
222 | 012 | 111 | 000
333 | 222 | 012 | 111
333 | 222 | 121 | 000

Cello

26. Three-Leaf Clover
(Start on the D String. "A" means Open A.)

333 | 013 | 111 | AAA
333 | 013 | 111 | 000
444 | 333 | 013 | 111
444 | 333 | 131 | 000

Bass

26. Three-Leaf Clover

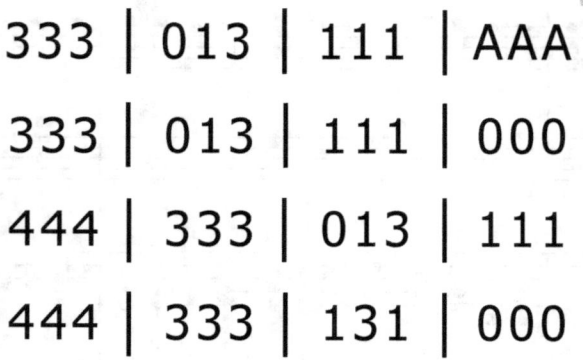

D string: 444 | 014 | 111   G string: 111
D string: 444 | 014 | 111 | 000
G string: 000   D string: 444 | 014 | 111
G string: 000   D string: 444 | 141 | 000

Learning the Violin, Viola, Cello, and Bass Score, Book One

Instrumental Books: #26, Page 23: **Bottom**
Piano Accompaniment

26. Three-Leaf Clover (on D to play together)

©2015 C. Harvey Publications All Rights Reserved.

Instrumental Books: #26, Page 23: **Bottom**
Piano Accompaniment

Three-Leaf Clover (on A for Violins and Violas)

Learning the Violin, Viola, Cello, and Bass Score, Book One

Instrumental Books: #27, Page 24: **Top**

Violin

27. Falling Down!
(on the D String if playing in a class)

2210 | 3321 | 2012 | 1 𝄽 1 𝄽

2210 | 3321 | 0211 | 0 𝄽 0 𝄽

Viola

27. Falling Down!
(on the D String if playing in a class)

2210 | 3321 | 2012 | 1 𝄽 1 𝄽

2210 | 3321 | 0211 | 0 𝄽 0 𝄽

Cello

27. Falling Down!
(on the D String if playing in a class.)

3310 | 4431 | 3013 | 1 𝄽 1 𝄽

3310 | 4431 | 0311 | 0 𝄽 0 𝄽

Bass

27. Falling Down!

D string | G string D string
4410 | 0041 | 4014 | 1 𝄽 1 𝄽

D string | G string D string
4410 | 0041 | 4014 | 1 𝄽 1 𝄽

©2015 C. Harvey Publications All Rights Reserved.

Instrumental Books: #27, Page 24: **Top**
Piano Accompaniment

27. Falling Down (on D to play together)

©2015 C. Harvey Publications All Rights Reserved.

Learning the Violin, Viola, Cello, and Bass Score, Book One

Instrumental Books: #27, Page 24: **Top**
Piano Accompaniment

Falling Down (on A for Violins and Violas)

©2015 C. Harvey Publications All Rights Reserved.

Instrumental Books: #28, Page 24: **Bottom**

Violin

28. Waltz
(on the D String if playing in a class)

012 | 333 | 210 | 111

012 | 321 | 232 | 111

012 | 333 | 210 | 111

012 | 333 | 221 | 000

Viola

28. Waltz
(on the D String if playing in a class)

012 | 333 | 210 | 111

012 | 321 | 232 | 111

012 | 333 | 210 | 111

012 | 333 | 221 | 000

Cello

28. Waltz
(on the D String if playing in a class.)

013 | 444 | 310 | 111

013 | 431 | 343 | 111

013 | 444 | 310 | 111

013 | 444 | 331 | 000

Bass

28. Waltz

D string | G string | D string

014 | 000 | 410 | 111

D string | G string D string

014 | 041 | 414 | 111

D string | G string | D string

014 | 000 | 410 | 111

D string | G string | D string

014 | 000 | 441 | 000

©2015 C. Harvey Publications All Rights Reserved.

Learning the Violin, Viola, Cello, and Bass Score, Book One

Instrumental Books: #28, Page 24: **Bottom**
Piano Accompaniment

28. Waltz (on D to play together)

©2015 C. Harvey Publications All Rights Reserved.

Instrumental Books: #28, Page 24: **Bottom**
Piano Accompaniment

Waltz (on A for Violins, Violas, and Cellos)

Learning the Violin, Viola, Cello, and Bass Score, Book One　　61

Instrumental Books: #29, Page 25: **Top**

Violin

29. Reaching Saturn
(on the D String if playing in a class)

012 | 210 | 123 | 3 𝄽 𝄽

123 | 321 | 234 | 4 𝄽 𝄽

432 | 234 | 321 | 1 𝄽 𝄽

321 | 123 | 210 | 0 𝄽 𝄽

Viola

29. Reaching Saturn
(on the D String if playing in a class)

012 | 210 | 123 | 3 𝄽 𝄽

123 | 321 | 234 | 4 𝄽 𝄽

432 | 234 | 321 | 1 𝄽 𝄽

321 | 123 | 210 | 0 𝄽 𝄽

Cello

29. Reaching Saturn
(Start on the D String. "A" means Open A.)

013 | 310 | 134 | 4 𝄽 𝄽

134 | 431 | 34A | A 𝄽 𝄽

A43 | 34A | 431 | 1 𝄽 𝄽

431 | 134 | 310 | 0 𝄽 𝄽

Bass

29. Reaching Saturn

D string ──────────── G string
0 1 4 | 4 1 0 | 1 4 0 | 0 𝄽 𝄽
D string G string D string G string

1 4 0 | 0 4 1 | 4 0 1 | 1 𝄽 𝄽
G string D string G string D string

1 0 4 | 4 0 1 | 0 4 1 | 1 𝄽 𝄽
G string D string G string D string

0 4 1 | 1 4 0 | 4 1 0 | 0 𝄽 𝄽

©2015 C. Harvey Publications All Rights Reserved.

Instrumental Books: #29, Page 25: **Top**
Piano Accompaniment

29. Reaching Saturn (on D to play together)

©2015 C. Harvey Publications All Rights Reserved.

Instrumental Books: #29, Page 25: **Top**
Piano Accompaniment

Reaching Saturn (on A for Violins and Violas)

Instrumental Books: #30, Page 25: **Bottom**

Violin

30. Back to Earth
(on the D String if playing in a class)

0210 | 1111 | 1321 | 2222

2012 | 3333 | 2312 | 0000

Viola

30. Back to Earth
(on the D String if playing in a class)

0210 | 1111 | 1321 | 2222

2012 | 3333 | 2312 | 0000

Cello

30. Back to Earth
(on the D String if playing in a class.)

0310 | 1111 | 1431 | 3333

3013 | 4444 | 3413 | 0000

Bass

30. Back to Earth
(Start on the D string. "G" means open G.)

0410 | 1111 | 1G41 | 4444

4014 | GGGG | 4G14 | 0000

©2015 C. Harvey Publications All Rights Reserved.

Instrumental Books: #30, Page 25: **Bottom**
Piano Accompaniment

30. Back to Earth (on D to play together)

Back to Earth (on A for Violins, Violas, and Cellos)

©2015 C. Harvey Publications All Rights Reserved.

Instrumental Books: #31, Page 26: **Top**

Violin

31. Neptune
(on the D String if playing in a class)

2212 | 3323 | 2212 | 021𝄽

2212 | 3210 | 2232 | 120𝄽

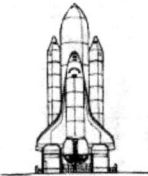

Viola

31. Neptune
(on the D String if playing in a class)

2212 | 3323 | 2212 | 021𝄽

2212 | 3210 | 2232 | 120𝄽

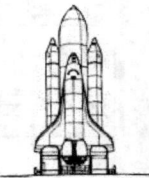

Cello

31. Neptune
(On the D String if playing in a class.)

3313 | 4434 | 3313 | 031𝄽

3313 | 4310 | 3343 | 130𝄽

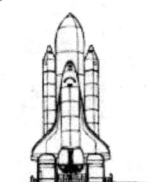

Bass

31. Neptune
(Start on the D string. "G" means open G.)

4414 | GG4G | 4414 | 041𝄽

4414 | G410 | 44G4 | 140𝄽

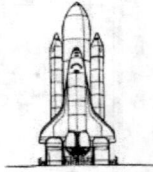

©2015 C. Harvey Publications All Rights Reserved.

Learning the Violin, Viola, Cello, and Bass Score, Book One

Instrumental Books: #31, Page 26: **Top**
Piano Accompaniment

31. Neptune (on D to play together)

©2015 C. Harvey Publications All Rights Reserved.

Instrumental Books: #31, Page 26: **Top**
Piano Accompaniment

Neptune (on A for Violins, Violas, and Cellos)

Instrumental Books: #32, Page 26: **Bottom**

Violin

32. Flying Away
(on the D String if playing in a class)

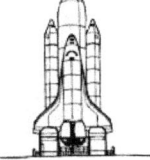

012 | 012 | 012 | 111

123 | 123 | 123 | 222

444 | 222 | 444 | 222

333 | 111 | 231 | 000

Viola

32. Flying Away
(on the D String if playing in a class)

012 | 012 | 012 | 111

123 | 123 | 123 | 222

444 | 222 | 444 | 222

333 | 111 | 231 | 000

Cello

32. Flying Away
(Start on the D String. "A" means Open A.)

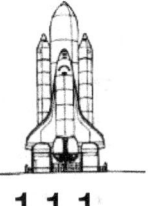

013 | 013 | 013 | 111

134 | 134 | 134 | 333

AAA | 333 | AAA | 333

444 | 111 | 341 | 000

Bass

32. Flying Away
(Start on the D string. "G" means open G.)

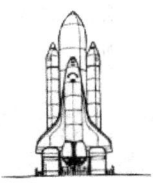

014 | 014 | 014 | 111

14G | 14G | 14G | 444

(G string) (D string) (G string) (D string)

111 | 444 | 111 | 444

GGG | 111 | 4G1 | 000

Instrumental Books: #32, Page 26: **Bottom**
Piano Accompaniment
32. Flying Away (on D to play together)

Learning the Violin, Viola, Cello, and Bass Score, Book One

Instrumental Books: #32, Page 26: **Bottom**
Piano Accompaniment

Flying Away (on A for Violins and Violas)

©2015 C. Harvey Publications All Rights Reserved.

Instrumental Books: #33, Page 27

Violin
33. Reading Music

This is a treble clef sign. The violin plays notes in treble clef. → This is a staff. It has 5 lines and 4 spaces. The notes go on the lines and in the spaces.

The music notes are placed on the lines and in the spaces to mean certain sounds.

Space Notes
Dried
Fish
All
Cats
Enjoy

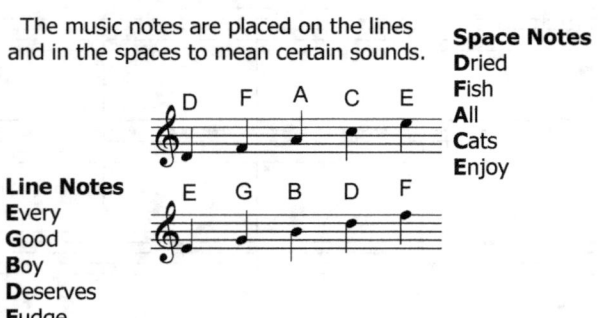

Line Notes
Every
Good
Boy
Deserves
Fudge

The notes go in order of the alphabet, from A to G, and then start back at A again.

Viola
Reading Music

This is an alto clef sign. The viola plays notes in alto clef. → This is a staff. It has 5 lines and 4 spaces. The notes go on the lines and in the spaces.

The music notes are placed on the lines and in the spaces to mean certain sounds.

Space Notes
Every
Good
Boy
Deserves
Fudge

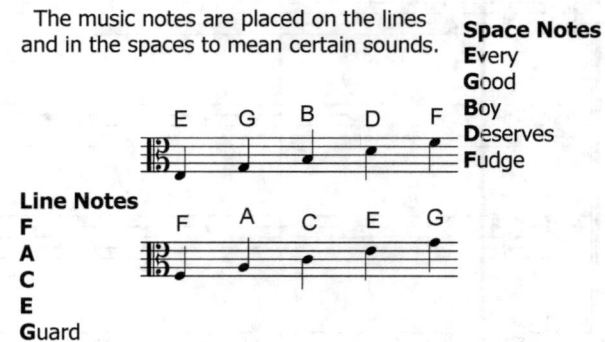

Line Notes
F
A
C
E
Guard

The notes go in order of the alphabet, from A to G, and then start back at A again.

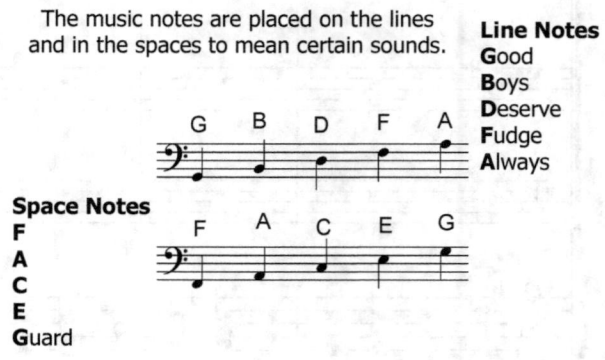

Cello
33. Reading Music

This is a bass clef sign. The cello plays notes in bass clef. → This is a staff. It has 5 lines and 4 spaces. The notes go on the lines and in the spaces.

The music notes are placed on the lines and in the spaces to mean certain sounds.

Line Notes
Good
Boys
Deserve
Fudge
Always

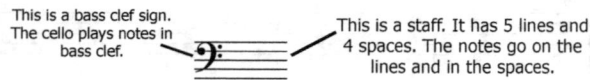

Space Notes
F
A
C
E
Guard

The notes go in order of the alphabet, from A to G, and then start back at A again.

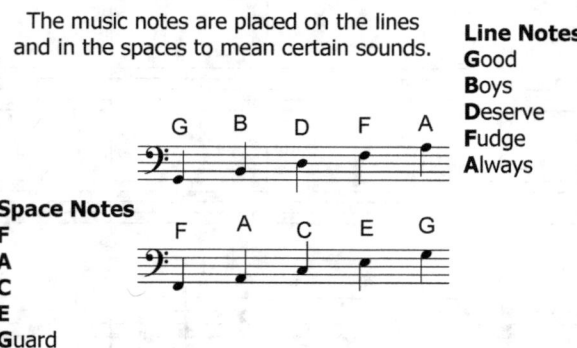

Bass
33. Reading Music

This is a bass clef sign. The bass plays notes in bass clef. → This is a staff. It has 5 lines and 4 spaces. The notes go on the lines and in the spaces.

The music notes are placed on the lines and in the spaces to mean certain sounds.

Line Notes
Good
Boys
Deserve
Fudge
Always

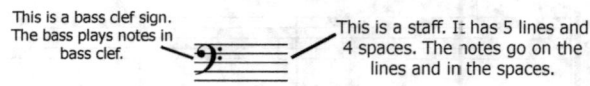

Space Notes
F
A
C
E
Guard

The notes go in order of the alphabet, from A to G, and then start back at A again.

©2015 C. Harvey Publications All Rights Reserved.

Instrumental Books: #34, Page 28

34. Counting

♩ This is a quarter note.
Hold it for 1 count.

𝅗𝅥 This is a half note.
Hold it for 2 counts.

𝅝 This is a whole note.
Hold it for 4 counts.

♪ This is an eighth note.
Hold it for 1/2 a count.

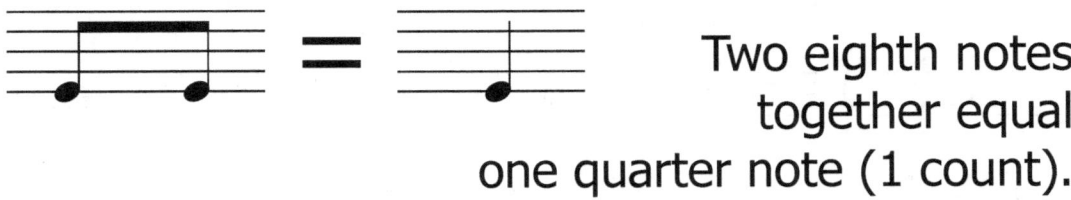

Two eighth notes together equal one quarter note (1 count).

Learning the Violin, Viola, Cello, and Bass Score, Book One

Instrumental Books: #35, Page 29
#36, Page 30
#37, Page 31

Note: Student books have accidentals written for all F-sharps and C-sharps, instead of key signatures, to build an early awareness of notes and note names.

35. A and B on the A String

36. A, B, and C# on the A String

37. A, B, C#, and D on the A String

©2015 C. Harvey Publications All Rights Reserved.

Instrumental Books: #38, Page 32

38. Boil Them Cabbage Down

Instrumental Books: #39, Page 32

39. Long-Short-Short Cabbage

Learning the Violin, Viola, Cello, and Bass Score, Book One

Instrumental Books: #40, Page 33

40. Half Notes Get Two Counts

©2015 C. Harvey Publications All Rights Reserved.

78 Learning the Violin, Viola, Cello, and Bass Score, Book One

Instrumental Books: #41, Page 33

41. Mississippi Hot Dogs with Cabbage

©2015 C. Harvey Publications All Rights Reserved.

Learning the Violin, Viola, Cello, and Bass Score, Book One 79

Instrumental Books: #42, Page 34

42. Miss Mary Mack

©2015 C. Harvey Publications All Rights Reserved.

Instrumental Books: #43, Page 35
#44, Page 36

43. D and E on the D String

44. D, E, and F♯ on the D String

©2015 C. Harvey Publications All Rights Reserved.

45. D, E, F#, and G on the D String

82 Learning the Violin, Viola, Cello, and Bass Score, Book One

Instrumental Books: #46, Page 38

46. Pickle Juice, Pickle Juice

©2015 C. Harvey Publications All Rights Reserved.

Instrumental Books: #47, Page 38

47. Pickle Juice Stomp

84

Instrumental Books: 48, Page 39

48. Peanut Butter Pie Pickle Juice

©2015 C. Harvey Publications All Rights Reserved.

Instrumental Books: #49, Page 40

49. The Rattle Sna-wa-wake

Instrumental Books: #50, 51, Page 41

50. The A String and the D String
(D and G for Bass)

51. Playing on D and A

Learning the Violin, Viola, Cello, and Bass Score, Book One

Instrumental Books: #52, Page 42

52. Who's that Knocking at my Window?

88

Instrumental Books: #53, Page 42

53. Pounding at the Window!

Instrumental Books: #54, Page 43

54. Tapping at the Window

Instrumental Books: "Basses Learn to Shift to 3rd Position" (Bass Book Only, page 44) #55, 56, Page 44

Basses Learn to Shift to 3rd Position
(only in the Bass book)

55. The D Major Scale

56. Super Challenge!

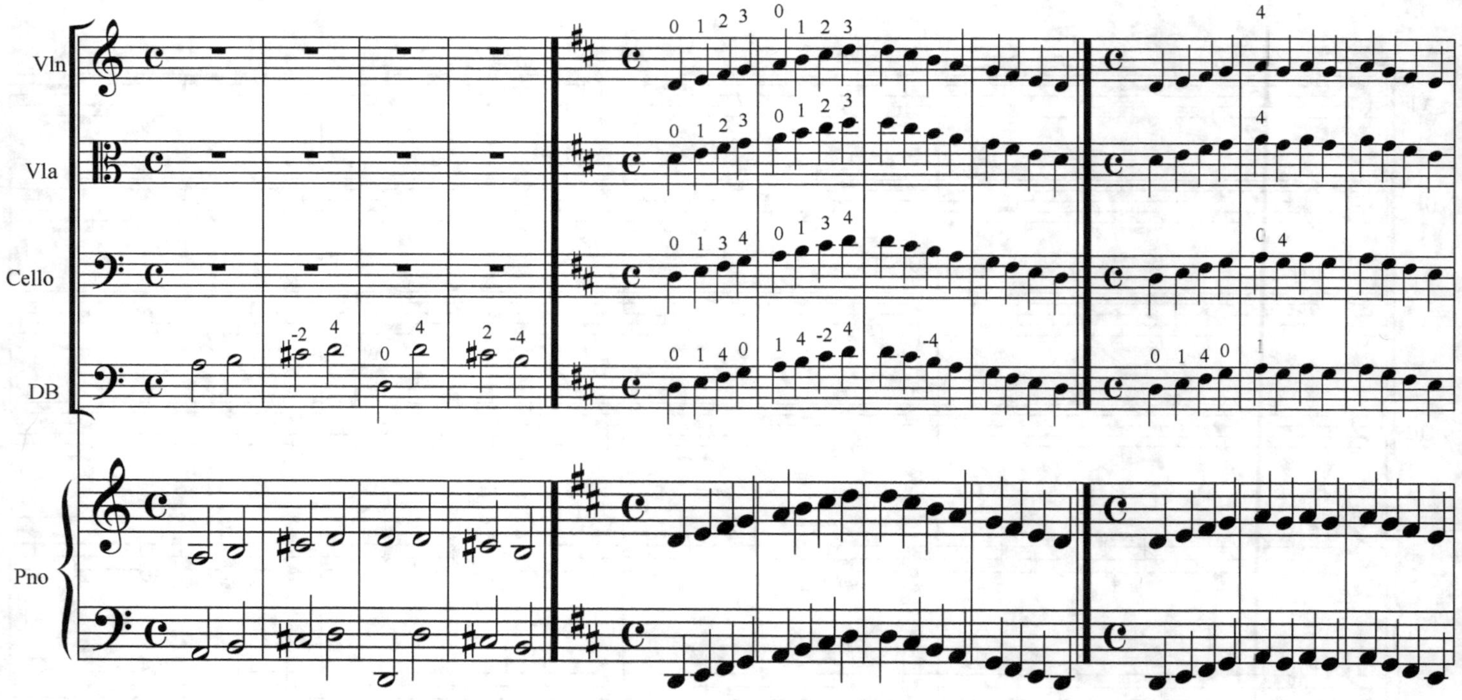

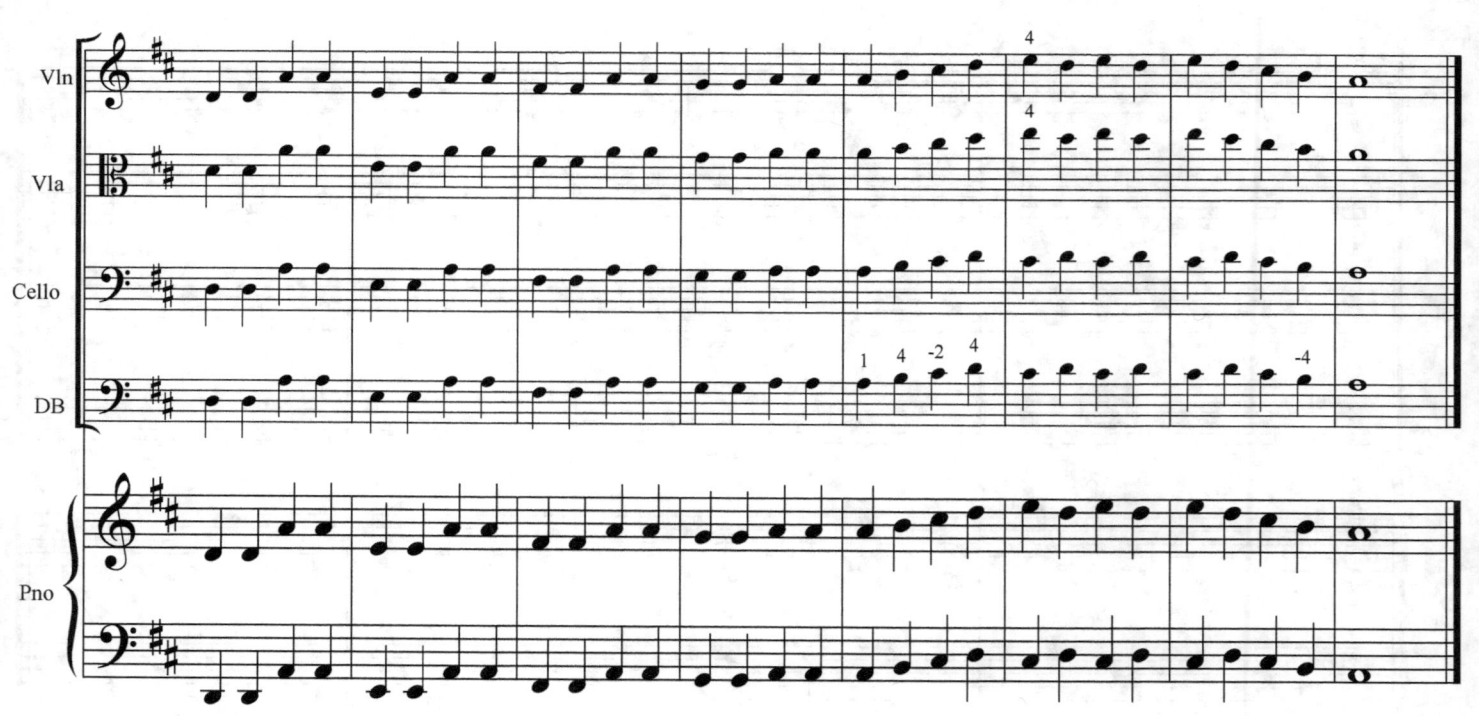

Learning the Violin, Viola, Cello, and Bass Score, Book One

Instrumental Books: #57, Page 45

57. Twinkle, Twinkle, Little Star

©2015 C. Harvey Publications All Rights Reserved.

92

Instrumental Books: #58, Page 46

58. Twinkle, Twinkle (Mississippi Hot Dog)

©2015 C. Harvey Publications All Rights Reserved.

Learning the Violin, Viola, Cello, and Bass Score, Book One

(Instrumental Books: #58, Page 46, cont.)

©2015 C. Harvey Publications All Rights Reserved.

Instrumental Books: "Basses Learn to Shift to 3rd Position on D" (Bass Book Only, page 47) #59, Page 47

Basses Learn to Shift to 3rd Position on D (only in the Bass book)

59. Ode to Joy

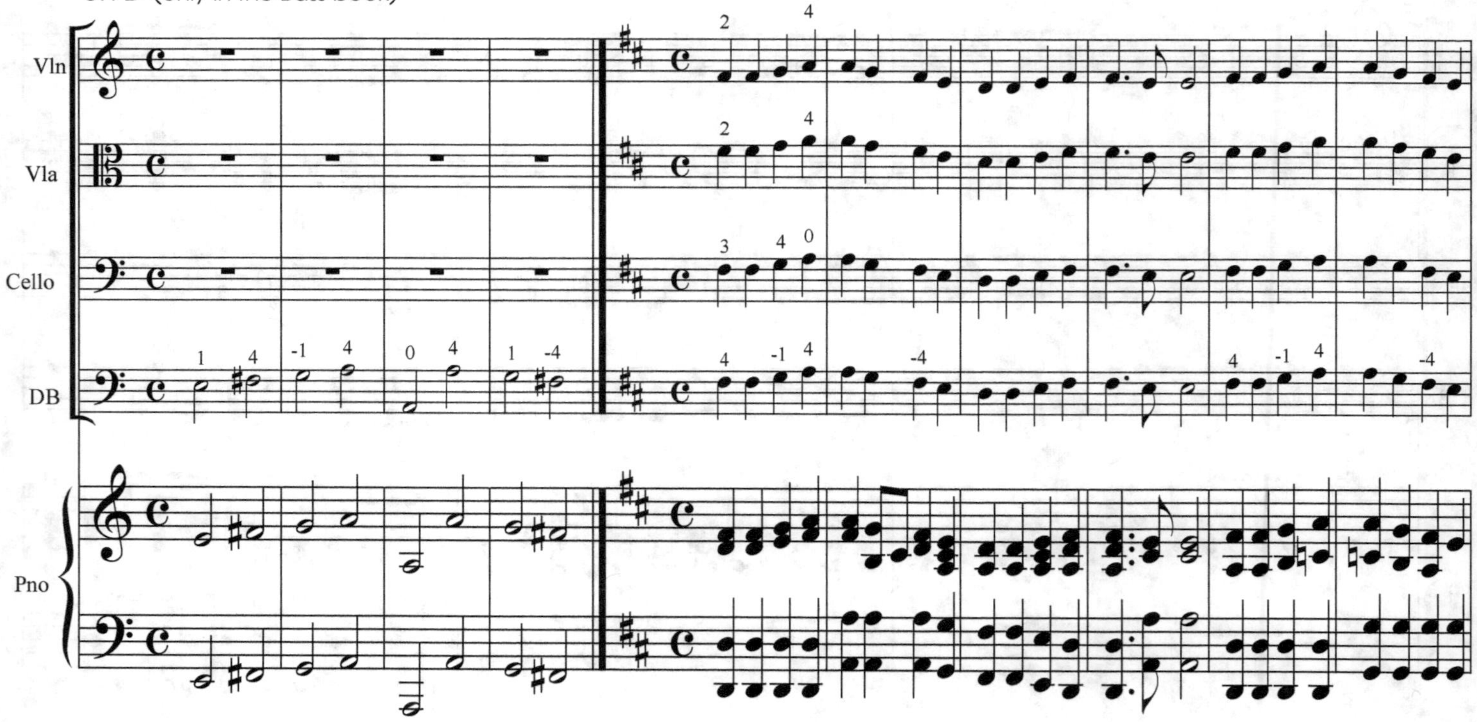

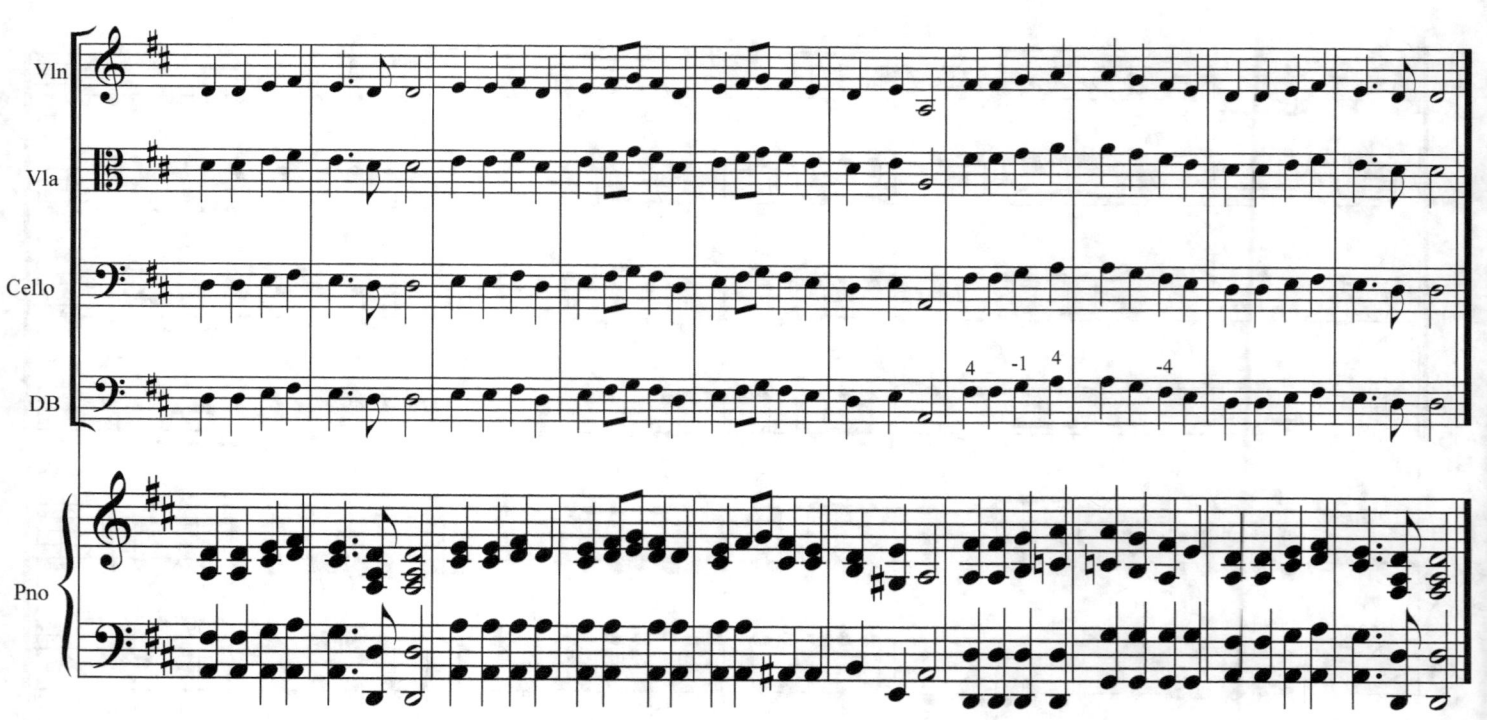

Learning the Violin, Viola, Cello, and Bass Score, Book One

Instrumental Books: #60, Page 48

60. Fulton Had a Steamboat

©2015 C. Harvey Publications All Rights Reserved.

Instrumental Books: #61, Page 48

61. Pickle Juice Steamboat

Learning the Violin, Viola, Cello, and Bass Score, Book One   97

Instrumental Books: #62, Page 49

62. Blueberry Steamboat

©2015 C. Harvey Publications All Rights Reserved.

Instrumental Books: #63, Page 49

63. Mississippi Hot Dog Steamboat

Instrumental Books: #64, Page 50

64. Jingle Bells

Instrumental Books: #65, Page 51

65. Dreidel Song

Instrumental Books: #66, Page 52

66. The Bears Went Over the Mountain

Instrumental Books: #67, Page 53

67. Scotland's Burning
(to learn in unison)

This page left blank to facilitate page turns.

Instrumental Books: #67, Page 53

Scotland's Burning
(as a Round)

Learning the Violin, Viola, Cello, and Bass Score, Book One

(Instrumental Books: #67, Page 53, cont.)

Learning the Violin, Viola, Cello, and Bass Score, Book One

Instrumental Books: #68, Page 54

68. Old MacDonald

©2015 C. Harvey Publications All Rights Reserved.

Instrumental Books: #69, Page 55

69. London Bridge

Instrumental Books: #70, Page 56

70. Cotton-Eyed Joe

Learning the Violin, Viola, Cello, and Bass Score, Book One

Instrumental Books: #71, Page 56

71. Mississippi Hot Dog Joe

©2015 C. Harvey Publications All Rights Reserved.

Instrumental Books: #72, Page 57

72. Blueberry Joe

Instrumental Books: #73, Page 57

73. Blueberry Pickle Juice Joe

Instrumental Books: #74, Page 58

74. Frère Jacques
(to learn in unison)

Learning the Violin, Viola, Cello, and Bass Score, Book One 113

Instrumental Books: #74, Page 58

Frere Jacques
(as a Round)

©2015 C. Harvey Publications All Rights Reserved.

114
Learning the Violin, Viola, Cello, and Bass Score, Book One

Instrumental Books: #75, 76, Page 59

75. E and F# on the E String

76. E, F#, and G# on the E String

©2015 C. Harvey Publications All Rights Reserved.

Instrumental Books: #77, 78, Page 60

77. E, F#, G#, and A on the E String

78. E, F#, G#, A, and B on the E String

116 Learning the Violin, Viola, Cello, and Bass Score, Book One

Instrumental Books: #79, 80, Page 61

79. The Grey Goose

80. A Goosey Variation

©2015 C. Harvey Publications All Rights Reserved.

Instrumental Books: #81, Page 62

81. Pop Goes the Weasel

Instrumental Books: #82, Page 63

82. French Folk Song
(Violins have the melody, other instruments have harmony)

Learning the Violin, Viola, Cello, and Bass Score, Book One

(Instrumental Books: #82, Page 63, cont.)

Instrumental Books: #83, Page 64

83. French Folk Song
(Violas, Cellos, and Basses have the melody, Violins have the harmony)

Learning the Violin, Viola, Cello, and Bass Score, Book One

(Instrumental Books: #83, Page 64, cont.)

Instrumental Books: #84, Page 65

84. Allegro, by Anonymous

Learning the Violin, Viola, Cello, and Bass Score, Book One   123

(Instrumental Books: #84, Page 65, cont.)
#85, Page 66

85. G and A on the G String

©2015 C. Harvey Publications All Rights Reserved.

Instrumental Books: #86, Page 66
#87, Page 67

86. G, A, and B on the G String

87. G, A, B, and C on the G String

Learning the Violin, Viola, Cello, and Bass Score, Book One   125

Instrumental Books: #88, Page 67
#89, Page 68

88. G, A, B, and C on the G String

89. A-Hunting We Will Go

©2015 C. Harvey Publications All Rights Reserved.

126

Instrumental Books: #90, Page 69

90. River Train

This page left blank
to facilitate page turns.

Instrumental Books: #91, Page 70

91. Dvorak's Largo

Learning the Violin, Viola, Cello, and Bass Score, Book One

(Instrumental Books: #91, Page 70, cont.)

Dvorak's Largo, cont.

©2015 C. Harvey Publications All Rights Reserved.

Learning the Violin, Viola, Cello, and Bass Score, Book One

Instrumental Books: #92, 93, Page 71

92. C and D on the C String

93. C, D, and E on the C String

©2015 C. Harvey Publications All Rights Reserved.

Instrumental Books: #94, 95, Page 72

94. C, D, E, and F on the C String
(Basses Learn F♮)

95. C, D, E, F, and G on the C String
(Basses Learn F♮ and G)

Instrumental Books: #96, Page 73

96. Hammer Ring

Learning the Violin, Viola, Cello, and Bass Score, Book One

Instrumental Books: #97, Page 73

97. Won't You Ring, Old Hammer?

Instrumental Books: #98, Page 74

98. Yankee Doodle

Instrumental Books: #99, Page 75

99. Spider Song

Violin Finger Charts, Page 76

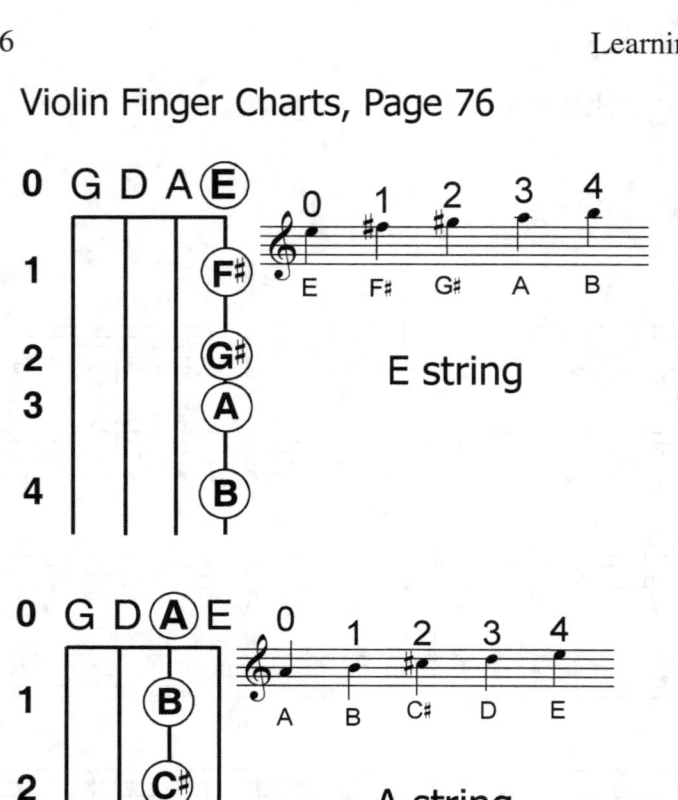

Violin Finger Charts, Page 77

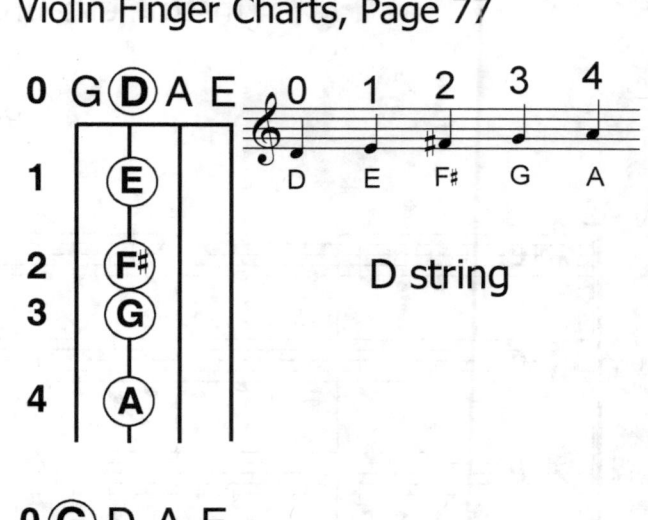

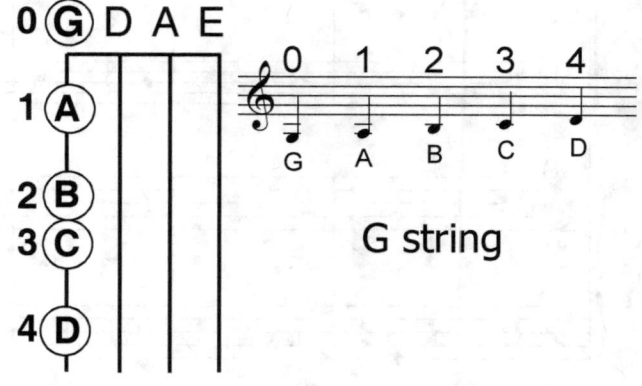

Viola Finger Charts, Page 76

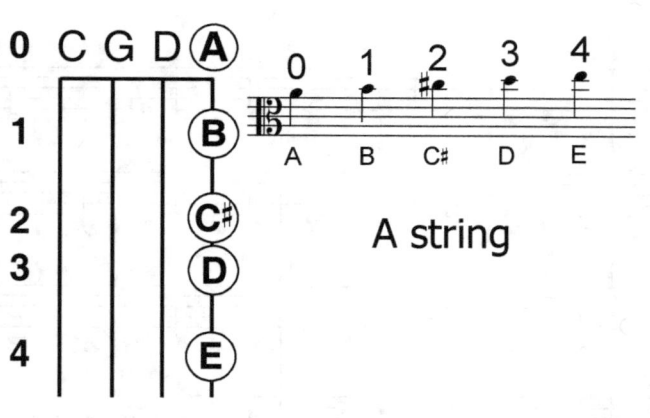

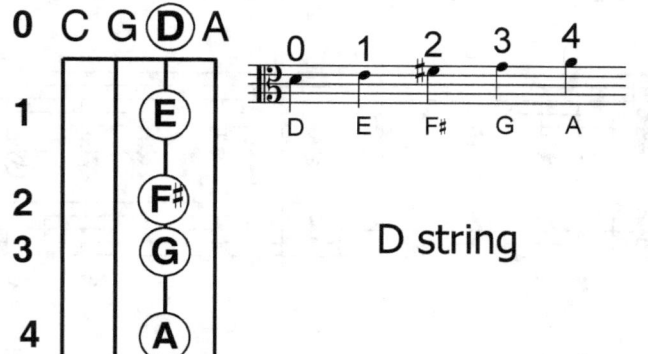

Viola Finger Charts, Page 77

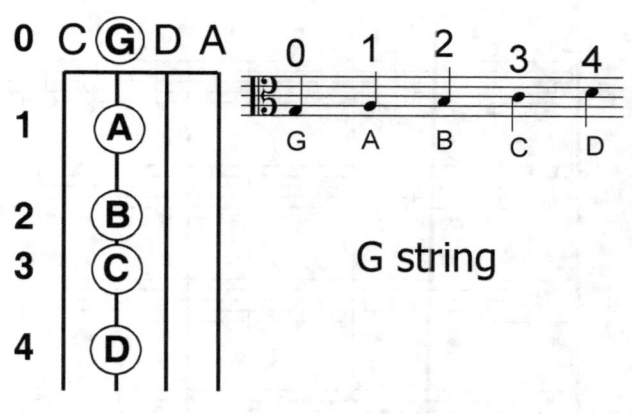

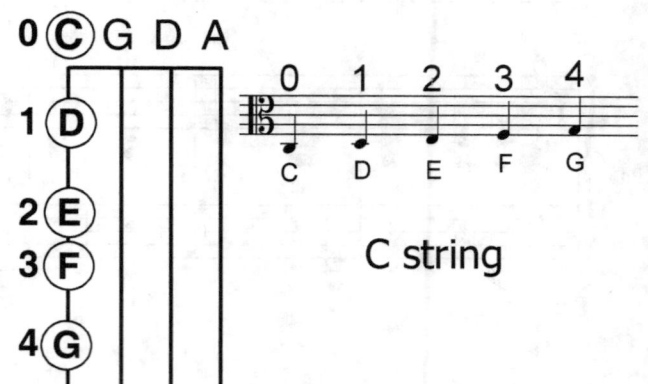

©2015 C. Harvey Publications All Rights Reserved.

Learning the Violin, Viola, Cello, and Bass Score, Book One   137

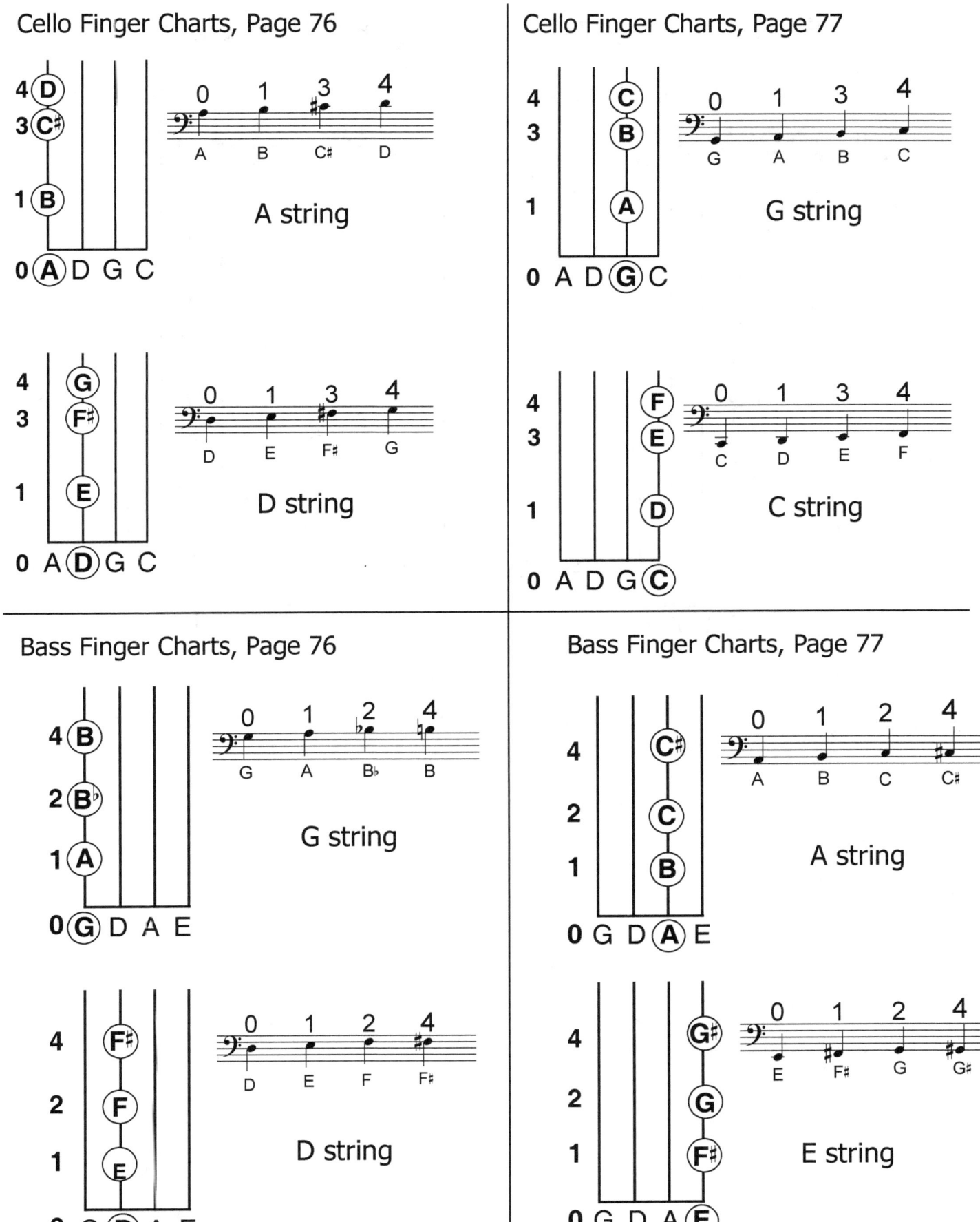

©2015 C. Harvey Publications All Rights Reserved.

Bass Finger Charts, Page 78

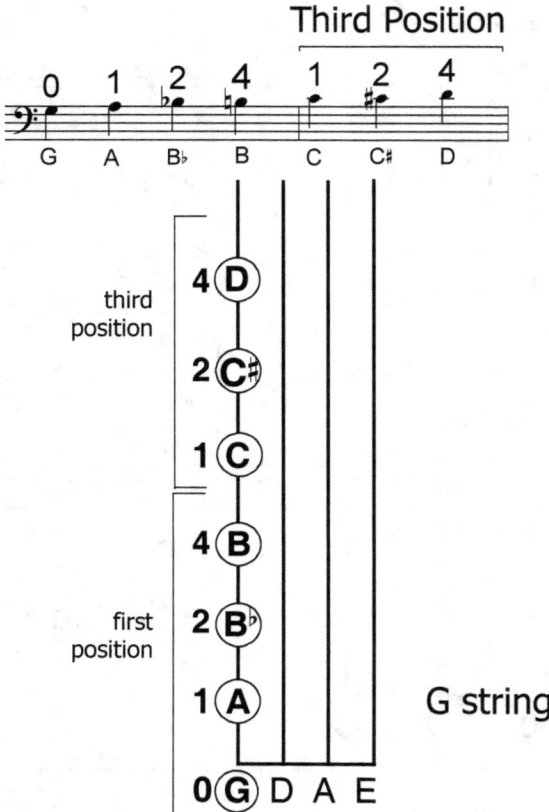

Bass Finger Charts, Page 79

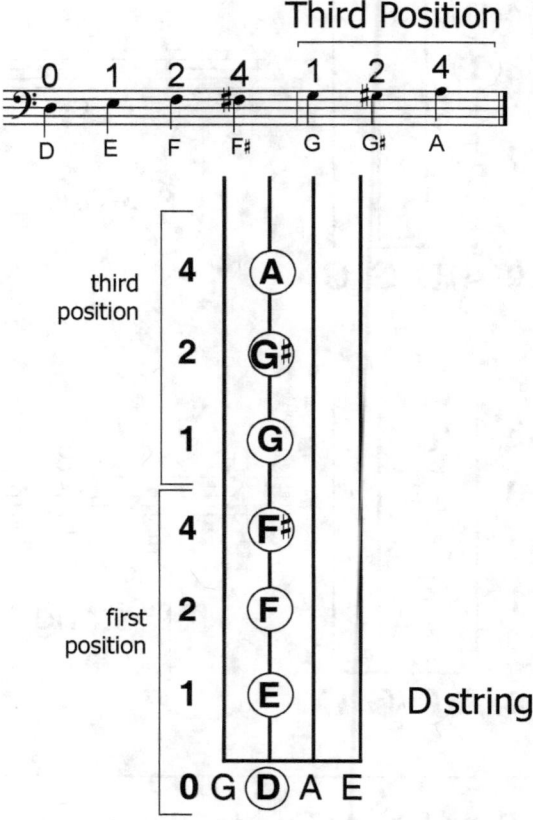

also available from **www.charveypublications.com**:

Learning the Violin, Book Two: CHP285

Can be used for
individual study, ***single-string classes***,
or ***mixed-string classes***, with:

Learning the Viola, Book Two: CHP286

Learning the Cello, Book Two: CHP287

Learning the Bass, Book Two: CHP288

Learning the Violin, Viola, Cello, and Bass, Book Two, Score: CHP289

also available from **www.charveypublications.com**:

Getting in Shape for Violin: CHP123

a multi-level string class book: "A" pages are in first position and can be played along with "B" pages that are slightly more difficult. Great for classes with players of different abilities. Violin, viola, cello, and bass books can be played together.

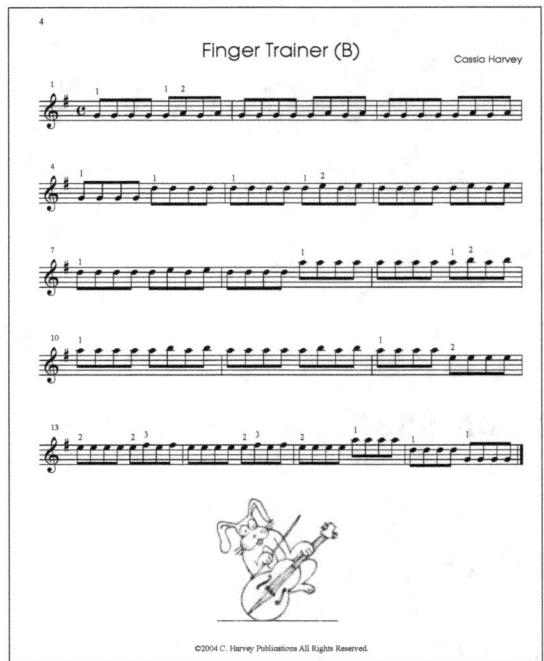

Can be used for *individual study*, *single-string classes*, or *mixed-string classes*, with:

Getting in Shape for Viola: CHP124
Getting in Shape for Cello: CHP125
Getting in Shape for Bass: CHP126

www.ingramcontent.com/pod-product-compliance
Lightning Source LLC
Chambersburg PA
CBHW051414070526
44584CB00023B/3427